untold.
secrets from the soul

Poetry by Bushra Zahid

ISBN: 978-1838114978

Copyright © 2021 Bushra Zahid
Cover Illustration & Interior Art by Bushra Zahid
Cover Design by Soulful Group

Bushra Zahid asserts the moral right under the Copyright, Designs and Patents Act 1988 to be identified as the author of this work.

All rights reserved. No part of this publication may be reproduced, stored in a retrieval system, or transmitted, in any form or by any means without prior written consent of the author, nor be otherwise circulated in any form of binding or cover other than that in which it is published and without a similar condition being imposed on the subsequent purchaser.

This edition was published by the Soulful Group in 2021.

"We unlace words & detangle life to help make the world a more soulful place".

www.soulfulgroup.com

acknowledgments.

By the grace of Allah (God).

Thank you to everyone who is taking the time to read this book. May Allah fill your life with joy and blessings. I hope you can somewhat relate to the poems, or better still, understand the emotional depth I am trying to convey.

Never in my life would I have thought I'd write a book, but here we are. Of course, this would have been impossible without all my family and friends.

A huge thank you to my mother, for being my role model and for being the strongest woman I know. Thank you to my dad for always being my best friend. Love and gratitude to my grandparents in the UK and my grandmother, who passed away in Pakistan - without their duas I'd be nothing.

Thank you Hafsa Api, who has also passed away, but has always remained in my heart. Gratitude to Lehba Api, Saima Api, all my Khala's, Mamo's, Erika Baji, and Julia Baji.

I'm extremely grateful for the support and guidance from Rosie at the Rainbows Hospice and Fiza; both of you are truly the best human beings and deserve the whole world. I remember when Fiza said that I should publish my poetry and I got extremely terrified, but she believed in me and supported me with my creative choices.

Thank you to my publisher, Shobana Baji for being such a kind human being, and for being so supportive of my poetry. She's made me feel so confident in what I wrote, and I can't wait to continue my creative journey.

Lastly, I cannot explain how blessed and grateful I feel towards Allah. If he didn't give me these physical and emotional challenges, I'd probably never even have something to write about. I know in some cultures, they believe that being physically different (disabled) is a curse, but I know that it is an absolute blessing. In the moment, we think that God is being so cruel but after the storm has gone, we realise 'why' we were placed in a particular situation. Thank you, Allah Swt, for blessing me with so much more than I could have asked for.

Api = sister or sister figure
Khala = auntie or auntie figure
Mamo = uncle or uncle figure
Baji = elder sister or elder sister figure
Duas = prayers or blessings

dedication.

To the person I fell in love with, thank you. You taught me about love, the beautiful side, and the bitter side. Without you, I wouldn't have realised my strength.

contents.

the truth hurts [7]

broken [14]

falling [29]

hidden from the moonlight [35]

good things never last [40]

guided by his light [52]

not in this lifetime [57]

the truth hurts.

AN ODE TO BULLEH SHAH

Agg lage vich seenay de
Seena thap ke vaang tandoor hoya
Kuch loogan diya tanhayan ne maar dita
Kuch saajan Akhaan toh door hoya

My chest has been set on fire
Now my chest is so hot it has become a stove
Some caused by people taunting me
And some caused by my lover being away
from my eyes

Ik sheesha laya si yaar wekhan layi
Oh vi zameen teh dig kar choor hoya, Bulleh
shah! Lokhi hass ke yaar mana lainde Sada
rona, vi nahi Moonzoor hoya

I had one mirror to see my lover
That mirror fell to the floor and smashed into
pieces
Bulleh Shah, people managed to woo their
lovers by laughing
Yet mine can´t even accept my tears

I AM A MONSTER

I feel my anxiety creeping in
Like a sinister sea
Desperate to drown me
I feel it deep in my chest
A heavy hammer lays camp in my heart

I feel nauseous
Like there's a hand
A hand that is climbing in my chest
Towards my throat
Ripping my breath to shreds

My tears sting
Like there's some venom mixed within it
There's a sinister part of me
That whispers horror-like things

> *What if you lose everything?*
> *What if something goes wrong?*
> *What if everyone starts hating you?*

It hisses and cackles at my vulnerability
It feeds on my weakness
I'm my own monster
And that monster part of me is seduced
Seduced by my own fear
My own anguish
My own tears

I don't need saving from anyone
I need saving from myself
Because my monstrous self
Is a sadist of self-anguish

A LETTER OF HONESTY

I think I need to be truthful to myself
I think I need to be honest with my heart
No lies, just the truth
No matter how bitter it may be

A part of me does want to live
I want to live for myself
Not just for the sake of my parents
Just for me

I need to find a reason to live though....

The thing that made me want to fly
The thing that made me want to survive the darkest storm
That belongs to someone else now

I need to accept that
But it's too hard
It's more bitter than any poison

I want to live for myself
But I know I can't
Because the reason has gone

And being honest?
I'm too tired to set myself on a journey of exhaustion

Knowing that there's a high chance of failure
Which is why I turn to death
Waiting for my next and last dream

Knowing that this will be there
Sooner or later
Knowing it'll never fail me
Satisfying my hunger for peace

LET ME DREAM FOR ONCE

I miss you, more than I ever could
Yet every time I pray to see you
you're with someone else
Why?
Why couldn't it be just you?
Why am I constantly reminded that you're someone else's?

My reality is bitter enough
Let me dream for once
It's the only way I can survive

My heart feels empty without you
The sun feels sharp without you
The rain feels heavy without you

My darkness scares me now
I'm used to it, but I want it gone
My tears suffocate me, I'm used to it
But I want them gone....

For once. Let me melt in his embrace
Let me feel ease
Just once...
Let me feel happy again
Because two years of darkness is quite some time
And I know there's many years

broken.

DEFEATED BY LIFE

They say life is short
And to live every moment of it
What if I told you...
What if told you my life is like an eternity?
What if I said that every moment feels like a never-ending death?
What if I told you...
That right now I want everything to end
Because my future was already predicted
Predicted by my condition
By my doctors
And by me
I know that I'll never be happy
Because in all my life
I had only one moment of genuine happiness
And that ended in the blink of an eye
My safety blanket got snatched away
What once was soft fur is now sharp as blades
Cutting through the thin layers of my heart
At times I fool myself
Thinking maybe there's a spot that has fur
But I lie
I just want this to end
If every day is going to be like harsh blocks of iron?
I'd rather die
Because I truly have nothing to live for
And I'm too exhausted
I admit it
Life has defeated me

I AM A LIAR

I'm a liar
I'm a great liar
I'm so good at lying
That I lie to myself
And believe it.

I told myself
Things will get better
It just will
Lie.

I told myself
This love will be worth it
With or without pain
Lie.

I told myself
One day things will change
And your strength will shine through
Lie!

I looked around the world to see who my
worst enemy was
Turns out
I just had to look at my reflection.

Did I really hate myself that much
That I fed myself false hopes
I told myself that this illusion is real
In reality, it was a vile vail to cover the truth.

The truth may be bitter
But it gets better by time
Why did I hide the truth?
Or did I have an addiction?

An addiction to destroy everything
Including myself.

IF YOU SAW MY SOUL

If you saw my soul
What would it look like?
If you could see my soul in a human form
What would it be like?
I'll tell you

My eyes would be dark
Numb as a poisonous ink
They'd be covered in bruises
Streaks of salty water marks, tattooed on my cheeks
They would be hollow, as if it's a skull...

My lips, busted from the corners
Oozing out blood, deep red blood
Showing all the deep anguish
Lifeless lips, not how they used to be

My petite neck, covered in bright hues of pink scratches
Some showing new traumas
Some showing old scars
Never to be healed again

My arms, my legs, my stomach
Crowded with deep bruises, sinister scars and brutal blood

And my heart ?
My heart ripped out my chest

A hole showing the brutality that has been inflicted
My heart hanging by just one small thread
Surrounded by hues of beastly black...

So this...

This is what my soul would look like in a human form
Scary right?
If my emotions were personified
This is what it would look like

Now do you see how much I'm struggling?
Or is that still not enough?

MATURITY

Sometimes, I think to myself
How did I end up here?
How did I survive this darkness?
They said I'd never enter adulthood
Yet I have

How?

Should I be grateful?
Or should I grieve?
Should I be happy that I have matured way
before my age?
Maybe it's to make up for the fact I might not
reach the life of an elderly?

I wish I could go back in time
To the times that were filled with love
A time full of true joy, laughter, and smiles
It feels like an eternity since I've felt that
An eternity since peace

Whatever, it is
I wanted freedom from pain
Not constantly helping others
With a heart terribly broken
By life

NOT MADE TO BE HAPPY

Why can't things be simple?
Just for once
There are always complications.
And I've had enough...

I'm absolutely Shattered

and exhausted

People have medical help to live and enjoy life
I have to live for the sake of medical help
Without that, I'd be dead
And that's what I really want

Because I never asked to live
I never asked to fight something
That shouldn't be fought for in the first place

If death means no pain?
I'm willing to die right now
Because all I want, is freedom

Why is it?
Why is it, that every time I let the light of happiness shine in my heart
It ends up burning my skin
It's like a sinister fire
hungry for the flesh of a broken soul

Why is it that the moonlight feels like ice?
Like the light pierces through my soul
Slicing my heart right open

Maybe... just maybe I'm not made for a joyful life

Maybe I have grown attached to my darkness
Like a child surrounded by darkness
It may be a horrible surrounding
But it doesn't know any other way

Maybe... just maybe
I'm not one of those people who are happy

Maybe I am merely a soul that is executed from the world of true happiness

SADISTIC MONSTER

I'm being dominated by my life
Burning iron shackles
Clutched around my throat
Venomous chains snaked around my wrists
Torturing me endlessly
Mocking my suffering

My life is standing in front of me
Staring at me with red beady eyes
A monster looking at its prey
Wanting to torment it like an animal's chew-toy

My life is right in front of me
The claws hold a whip
The whip of several traumas
Each whip stings like vinegar on a wound
Leaving blood full cuts
Opening the soft delicate skin
They are leaving marks, only I can see them
Or only I could reveal them to someone
But it's to repugnant
There's no one in the world who would want to see these injuries
Not even my own parents
I hoped that love would set me free
And it did
Until it changed sides

So here goes another day
Of constant whipping
And a broken numb soul
The key is in her hand
But she's so used to enduring this abuse
She doesn't know any other way to live
Like a bird in an open cage

So here goes another day of waiting
Waiting for death to take my hand
As if guiding an innocent child from abuse
And death would say to me:

I'm finally here to take you away my dear
Let me reunite you with your happiness
and hand you over to the keeper of the
heavens, earth, and the whole universe.

THE HEART'S INFECTION

There's an infection
An infection in my heart
And it slowly spread overtime

It started with a drop of emotion
Feeling a slight knife stabbing pain
Deep within my heart
Slowly letting in the germ of life

It then invited itself
Living in my heart
Causing tears to run down my cheeks
Slight, rushes of pain
Pain that no medication can take away

Then slowly...but carefully it crawled within my veins
Spreading like wildfire
Causing physical pain
Pain that is bearable
Yet tears run down like melted lava
But I never tell them the truth

Now when doctors prescribe me medication
For some reason it doesn't kill the discomfort
And they wonder why?
Everyone wonders why?
Except me
I've realised that it's the heart's infection.
And that?
That has no cure but death

TONIGHT

Tonight, I've had enough
All of my chains broke
Making me lose my strength
Making me vulnerable and weak
For years I kept trying
Trying to keep myself upright
To hide away from my nasty scars
To pretend 'not seeing' the warnings
Yet they were completely clear

Tonight realisation has hit
Tonight I've realised that I've lost myself
I've lost myself to heartbreak, to love, to darkness
Right now I feel like I won't make it alive
And I don't want to
Tonight, I want peace, internal peace
Even if that means beneath the cold earth
Beneath the green grass
Protected from all humans
Safe and far from the feeling love...

Here lays the girl who died trying to find happiness

Tonight, I have been destroyed
By the hands of love
By the hands of belief
By the hands of hope

Ironic, isn't it?
Hope keeps people alive
My hope killed me
Caused me to die
Because tonight

I have died internally...

R.I.P

WORSE THAN IT IS

I have this fear
Clawing at my soul
Clinging on to me
As if it feeds on my emotions

I have this fear
Fear of the future
What if I lose who I am?
What if I'm not good enough?

I have this tiredness
Tiredness of life
Of a love that I treasure
When really it is venom

I want things to change
I want to get rid of the pain
But what if?
What if it's going to be worse than it is?

falling.

HUNGER FOR YOUR PRESENCE

There are days where I want you so bad
I'm like a fish without water
Trying to find a way to survive
Trying to fight the vulnerability

Some days, I lose control
I just need to be in your arms
I need to melt away in your embrace
Forgetting about the world
Forgetting about my pain

My reality is scary
It haunts my soul
Like a demon clinging onto a human
Never letting go
Yet you are like my saviour

Your name is like a powerful angel
Protecting me from myself
I just wish I could feel your presence
I wish I could feel your soul within me

Sometimes, when I dream of you
I feel like you're right here
I feel your soft lips on my cheeks
I feel your arms wrapped round my heart

And sometimes...for a little while
Your presence fills my hunger

MY PRECIOUS DIAMOND

Every time I see you, I hurt a little
It rips my soul to shreds
I'd do anything to make it go away
Even if I must sacrifice my happiness for you
Why do I do this to myself?

It's like you're a part of me
Like your soul is connected to mine
You get hurt, and I cry
You shed your precious tears
And my heart breaks into pieces

If only you were with me
I'd hold you close to me
I'd treat you like the most precious diamond in the world
A diamond that is worth more than anything

Because

you are my precious diamond

NEVER THE ONE TO LOVE

I used to find love foolish
I was never the one to love someone
I would be mortified by the word "kiss"
I'd be horrified by the thought of love

I'm never going to fall in love
I only love my family
How can you even sacrifice your own joy
for someone else?
How would you want to think about someone
who doesn't care about you?

Why would a smile by one person lighten
your heart?
Like the sun lives within you
How would that make you feel like you're
gliding in the air?
Like a bird enjoying the summer breeze

How would you want to kiss someone?
Why would you want to taste the sweetness
that they possess ?
Why would you want to be so close to
someone ?
So close that you're losing your sanity

I rolled my eyes as the mere thought came to
me

Little did I know
That sun shining
On March 23rd, 2016...

I'd lay my eyes on a boy
With Hazel eyes
And an angelic voice
Changing my life forever

And he'd Teach Me

                How

                To

                Love

YOU ARE MY WISH

Every wish I make
Your name is always there
No matter if it's a pray in front of God
Or simple wishes that people make up
It's always you

In every sajda (prostrating)
Your name is on my lips
Every birthday wish I make
The fire I blow out
Dances at the call of your name

Some people believe shooting stars are a curse from God
Some people believe a wish should be made
I believe in both
I still wish for you in the twinkling spark

Every breath I take
Calls out your name
Every song I hear, sounds like you
Every dream I see, I only feel you

hidden from the moonlight.

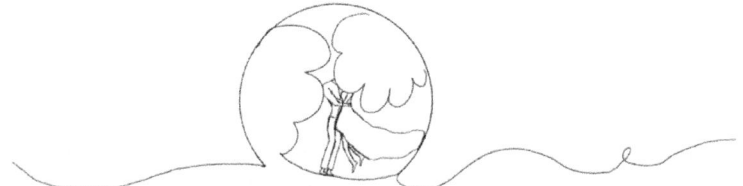

HOW CAN YOU MAKE ME FEEL?

How?

How can you make me feel this way?
How do you create a desire in me?

With just one look
All it takes is those honey brown eyes
One look at those eyes, and my heart flutters
Like a butterfly trying to escape a cage

Just stare makes weak
It makes me want to be at your mercy
How I want you to suffocate me
With your gaze

How I want to be trapped
Between those strong arms

How I'd want no space between us
Just your soul and mine
Making the moon blush
Your fingers intertwining in mine
Making sure I never escape

I'd never want to escape
I'd never want to escape

I never want to escape this torturous love

JEALOUSY

People say that it's an evil thing
It's sinister
How you'd wish destruction on someone
That's not true...

Well, I get a little sinister
A little fire burns in my soul
It's harmless, I swear
I just get random urges to capture you
To grab you by your shirt
And to never let you go

I want you to myself
No, I need you all to myself
Even if I have to tie you
So you never escape from my sight

Oh how I'd bite those lips
That sing oh so beautifully
How I'd love you...
Showing you that you're only mine
Making you only mine

Darling, it's all your fault
How dare you be so gorgeous
Inside and out
How dare you look like a Greek god

How dare you walk like a king
How dare you have a heart of gold
See how you drive me crazy?
You can't blame me, can you?

Darling, I'd do so much more to you
But I don't want to let them know
I'm still innocent in front of the world

LOVE ME PHYSICALLY

I've learnt almost everything about love emotionally
Now let me feel love physically

I've felt the crazy heartbeat
the anguish tears
The selfless sacrifices
The hope, of having you

Now I want to feel your burning gaze
I want to touch your soul
I want to taste that honey from your lips
I want to flush under your controlling gaze.

I want to bite my lip as you explore my heart
Finding places in me that never existed
I want to feel you caress every part of my soul...

Take me to that place where lovers go
Getting lost into each other
a firing passion between one another
Hold me tight against you, and don't let me escape

Let me be at your mercy
Take control of my breaths
And make me chant your name
Again, and again, and again...

good things never last.

ACCEPTANCE

I need to accept:
Accept the fact that your name will never be written in my fate
I'll never be the one you love so dearly
I'll never be the one to hear your voice early in the morning

I need to accept:
That I have to live without you
That you can't be my escape from reality
You can't be the cure for my pain
Because you're a medicine with a bad side effect

I need to accept:
That you belong to someone else
That you may love her
That she's the one you wake up with
She's the one in your arms
But can she love you more than me?
I don't think so

You don't even understand
You hurt me in every single way
But I cannot stop loving you

I HATE THE WAY I LOVE YOU

Why do I love you so much that it ends up killing me? It's like you're the only person I want to be with but, I want to let you go, I want to forget about you, but I just want you in my mind. You give me so many emotions at the same time. How is it even possible that you destroy me but don't realise. This just makes me hate the way I love you. You hurt me every time but like a fool I come back to you. I love you so much and that is making me hate you. You broke me, you left me vulnerable. But still for some hideous reason...

I don't want to give you up.

I NEVER KNEW LOVE WOULD HURT

I never knew love would hurt this much
I thought it was meant to be beautiful
Not like a serpent's tooth, sharp and painful
I thought taking my breath away would
mean a sigh of satisfaction
Not like a sea creature trying to survive
without water

It hurts, a lot, every breath feels like a stab
Every memory feels like a gunshot
Every moment feels like a bullet
Buried deep into my heart

A part of me wants to hate your entire
existence
Yet the more I want that, the ink of my
poisonous love deepens
Why ?
Why do your actions hurt me so much?
You're not even mine...

Why did I give you my heart and soul?
It's like I sent myself on a journey
Knowing that I'll never reach you...
I curse that day...
I curse that day when my eyes were first laid
upon you

I wish I could erase that moment in my life

But then again, without you?
I would be wondering around
Like a lost soul trying to find its way back
Knowing deep down, that it's never going to happen

WHAT IS LOVE?

What is love?

She wondered
Her eyes filled with curiosity
Portraying an innocence that couldn't be described

Is it the awe? The awe when you see stars living within his eyes?

Is it your heart beating insanely
The way he bites his lips when stuck in his thoughts? Or his laugh when trying to make a bad joke?

Is it the way his voice sends a chill down your spine?
Is it the loss of breath
The way his soft yet raspy voice sings?
Melting the inside of you, making you feel high

Alive

Or is the way he's just him?
The way he can express his emotions without being afraid
The way he knows how to be more human,
The way his flaws make him even more perfect?

Is that what love is?
She questioned in a haze
Like she got lost in him without even knowing

Yes, yes, it is - I spoke

But you forget that loving from afar has consequences. You forget that if you are not loved back, it kills...
It is another definition of destruction

You fall in love with every single part of him
His flaws are beautiful even when they can be dangerous as fire
You want him
No
You need him

Without him you feel empty
Like you've lost a part of you
A part that you'll never find
Not until you have him

When you see him with someone else
You're gone
You're constantly fighting a demon

You ask yourself
I should be happy that he's happy, right?
But I want him for myself
Am I being selfish?

With that, you destroy yourself for someone
For someone you love dearly
Yet they do not know you

So, people who find love
are lucky, so damn lucky

But we're the unfortunate ones
My love destroyed me
And you? You have only a few weeks left
Before you too get destroyed

She stared at me, with fear, with pain

I believe true love concurs all
How do you know that I'll be the same?

I smiled...

Because I am you

MY DARK FAIRY-TALE

I wish things were easy
For once I wouldn't have to suffer
I want the pain to go away
I want it to go away without unloving you
Because I know you're the cause of my suffering

Once upon a time
You used to be my fairy-tale
Now you've turned into a dark tale
Now you've changed me
I've changed into this sinister being
I'm addicted to this poison

I've gone so long without sunlight
I've withered into a dark creature
Now the sunlight burns my soul
The moonlight freezes my heart

Yet there's a small crack
Where the light seeps out
Calling out for help
Trying to save this damaged soul
But is it too late to be saved?
It may be a matter of time before that light fades away...

HARMFUL ADDICTION

I've never taken drugs
But if I had to guess what it'd feel like
I'd think of you

You're like my drug
Making me feel alive
Making me feel high
You're running through my veins
Creating sensations in my body
Sensations I never thought would exist
But addiction can be harmful right?

It can't be that bad
Not like I've felt like someone dragged me
Down into a pit of abyss
Not like I've felt huge amount of anguish
After you were with someone else
Nor did you ever make me cry to the point of
Wanting to rip my heart out

You didn't make my tears acidic
You didn't snatch my sanity away
I'm not like Harley Quinn, frantically trying
to find her lover
I'm not losing my mind at all
Not at all..
Not at all...

THE SUN AND THE MOON

My love story is like the sun and moon
A creation that can never meet at the same time
A creation that can be harmful if they unite

I'm like the sun
Bright, warm, dangerous
I can't wait for the evening
That's the only time I can get a glimpse of my moon
I have to push myself on the edge
Just so I can catch a small glimpse of you
Knowing that I'll never be able to touch you

You, the moon, beautiful as snow
Illuminating the night sky
Surrounded by your companions
Not knowing that there is a creation madly in love with you

You probably don't care
You're around the stars
Who love you so dearly
But they could never compete with my love
My love is stronger than the tiny stars combined together

But that doesn't matter
You don't even know I exist
And us meeting...
Can only cause destruction...

BETRAYAL

Sometimes,
Pain is so unbearable
That no words can describe the hurt

No tears can release the anguish
No scream can ease the frustration
No cry can ease the pain

People always talk about betrayal between eachother...
I betrayed myself
I betrayed myself for someone who constantly tortures me
He doesn't even know it

He mocks my pain with his innocent smile
He laughs at my tears with his soft laughter
He snatches my moments of peace with his romantic pictures
I fell for someone who's constantly torturing me

Thinking he'd heal my heart

guided by his light.

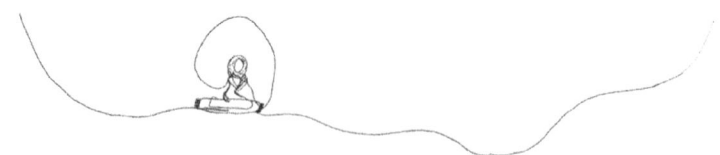

IF I COULD HEAR HIS WORDS

Oh God, why bring him into my life?
Why?
When you knew that he'd end up hurting me
Wasn't everything else enough?

She cried
As her hand raised in the air
Cupped as if she's holding a delicate creature
Her soul was standing on the soft pray mat
Pouring out her inner demons
In front of her lord

The room was in utter darkness
She was laying down
Yet her soul was fully worshiping him
protected by light
A noor (light) that could only be provided by
the creator himself

The world may see her as lonely and cold
But her creator saw her strength
A strong and brave human
That's why she was chosen

She was chosen to be in suffering
Because he knew
That without her being broken
She would not become an angel

She has made mistakes
but she shall be forgiven
For humans are not perfect at all
Fight this darkness my dear
For this will be the reason you will reach
your eternal paradise

Your siblings are safe with my angel
Your parents will be happy soon
And don't you worry
Your love will be with you soon too

There is no god but God, and Muhammad is
the messenger of God

As she finishes her pray
Gliding her hands over her face
As if she has carried the mercy of God within her hands
And pouring it over her broken soul

The sound of her breathing machine going
As her eyes slowly close

Ready for the next day....

OH JIBREEL (GABRIEL)

Once a wise angel said
Love whoever you want, in the end, you will leave them
But how is it that they left me?
Wasn't I the one meant to go?
I was the cause of suffering, right?
Shouldn't I be punished?
I was the cause of separation between a mother and her daughter
I was the cause of separation between a father and his son
Or is it that I'm the punishment for them
How bad must they have sinned to have me as their child?
Can't it be forgiven?

Oh, wise angel. Your God may be angry with me.
So please ask him... am I his true believer?
Or am I just a punishment that he sent to this world
Does he really love me?
Or am I just a punishment he created?
Oh Jibreel (A.s) I thought your lord loved all his people?
But wait... maybe I'm just a punishment
And that's why
I must see everyone I love... suffer
Forgive me my Lord...

IF I HAVE SINNED AGAIN

POWER OF MY FAST

The day I keep a fast
I feel safe
It may physically be tiring
But the hunger of my soul is satisfied
As if someone has managed to release the anguish within me

It's unusual
Because people may see it as self-harm
They may say, I'm too weak to fast
How do I explain that my fast feels like a safety net ?
How do I tell them that for once
The emotional pain doesn't hurt

My fast reminds me
That my broken soul can be at ease
It reminds me of the countless blessings bestowed upon me
It reminds me...
That Allah is always there for me

Ramadan is the purest month of all time
Our Lord cleanses the air within us
And we thrive to become better humans

not in this lifetime.

THE BOOK OF ILLUSIONS

Long ago someone gave me a book
I never asked for this book
Nor did I ever want it
Yet I had it in my hand

The book looked beautiful
Moulded to every person's liking
The people saw the book
They saw the cover how they wanted it to be seen
I, on the other hand, saw something else

Some saw fairy-tale covers
Surrounded by hues of gold, bright silver gems, and snowy pearls

Some saw simplicity
A plain cover with a simple title
And others, saw dark sinister covers

Me? What did I see?
I saw an old, ripped, dusty cover
Like it was pleading for mercy
Begging someone to help its torn parts

The pages were crumpled
Splatters of bloody ink
Lines, crying a river
The spine of the book bent
As if it endured several traumas

Now this is when I realised

This is the book of life
It's an illusion!
Why can't anybody see through this?

It baffled me, a lot
Why can't they see the truth?
Why can't they see the state of the book?

It's quite simple actually
Humans only see what they want to see
They prefer lies over honesty
Life is like a lie, filled with false promises
Death, on the other hand, is more honest
And that's why they don't like me
You prefer the truth
and that's why you saw the book in it's true form...

Your book is like you
Broken and torn
Yet people will see you as many other things
I'm sorry you must endure this book till I take it away
But our Maalik (king/Allah) knows best

Said malik-ul-maut (angel of death)

LIFE

I never understood why people think life is amazing
How they say:
- Live in the moment
- Enjoy the littlest things
- Life is beautiful
- Full of colours, light and honesty

How do I not see that?

Simple, because it doesn't exist
Correction, *it doesn't exist for me*

I tried savouring the moments of life
But they just turned bitter
Like the ocean's salt
From the outside, it may look beautiful
But once you're in the water
Coldness and drowning are all that exists

People don't know what goes on in my life
I don't know what goes on in theirs
All I need people to know is:
Some people aren't made to be happy

So, if a person let's their vulnerability out to you, don't tell them to live in the moment
Tell them that one day there will be a time
Where they will find some sort of peace
It just might not be in this world...And that's what I tell myself

YOU LEFT ME

There are days
Where I miss you so much
I want to rip my heart out
Days where your face flashes in front of my eyes
My memories drag me back to the time
The time where I saw you truly leave the world
You left me in this world
Alone

I was young
Afraid
Full of questions
Everyone was there
Everyone
But you

Why were you in a box?
Wrapped in the name of Allah's blanket
Why were you wearing blanket of white?
Why were your eyes closed?
Why is no one getting you out!?
Why was it that mum said that this is the last time I'd ever see you

Stop!
Help!
This is too much
As a twenty-year-old
Fear consumes me

And for a six-year-old?
It scarred me for life
And it shows

NOT THE WORLD

Some days, I feel like I'm on top of the world
As if I'm a ruthless queen
Like nothing could ever drag me down
And other days I feel so small
If the air would send a breeze
I'd just fade away

Sometimes, I feel like taking control
As if I'm a sly boss
Like power just lives within me
And other days I feel like an innocent infant
As if I want to be showered with warmth and hugs
Needing protected by the ones I love

I sometimes forget that it's okay
It's okay to want to lean on someone
It's okay to want to be loved
To want to rely on someone
To want to have my parents treating me like their little baby

All I need to remember is
I am strong no matter what
It's my choice if I want to dominate the world
Or if I want to just stay in the warmth of my own home
After all...I need to please myself
Not the world

A GUIDANCE TO USE PAIN AS A LADDER

Pain is like a step on a ladder
And that step is created by the creator himself
It' s a calling

And through namaaz (prostrating)
You'll be with him
Under his cloak
And it'll be a resting place for your soul
Preparing it to fight for the next battle

And once the battle is completed
You'll finally reach your paradise
Just hold on a little longer...

I can promise you
For your afterlife
It'll be worth it

author.

Bushra Zahid is a 20-year-old, with a flair for dark humour and spiritual clarity much beyond her years. She moved from Pakistan to the UK aged 18 months. She has experienced lifelong physical and medical challenges which seem only to fuel her creativity rather than inhibit her.

Instagram: **@iambushrazahid**

Printed in Great Britain
by Amazon